Maiden in the Mist
Collection of Poetry
By
Lee Fones

Poems by

Lee Fones

All poetry © Copyrighted poet Fones 2020

Special thanks to all my family, my writers group, photographers plus fantastic friends.

Misty Rose

Thick mist, Misty arose
From under, primrose
Misty so snowy white
Misty Rose took flight.

Down canal Misty flew
Misty Rose, damp dew
Underneath flickering light
Misty Rose, pure delight

In among prickly thorns
Boater's now tooting horns
Upon our canal, boaters go
Misty Rose wings do flow.

Misty Rose makes her ways
An elegant boat gently sways
Sways towards misty night
Misty Rose again takes flight.

Misty glides towards light fade
On our canal, Misty wade
Wading into misty twilight
Misty goes on her final flight.

Now this tale soon will end
Misty glides around a bend
Around bend to find last fish
Misty now glides a final swish.

Misty finally now asleep
Water silently does weep
Weeps away finally finished
Misty Rose, memory diminished.

Early Morning Mist

Early morning mist arises
 Sunday morning nice surprises
 In that mist, maiden rises, up!
 Upon coffee, she does, sup,

Elegantly, she proceeds.
In her coat varied tweeds
Going into woodland deep
To get a bit of extra sleep,

For, at last, it is a Sunday
It is a day before Monday,
Another week, an early rise,
'It is a poem full of surprise.

For snooze maidens, gone
On a Sunday up at one
Maiden arises up again
Even as it pours with rain,

Maiden now went to rest
Monday she'll be, stressed
Into office for more pay
So she can rest on a Sunday.

Fair Maiden

Maiden sat upon a log.
 Early morning misty fog.
 It was early, quite a haze.
 Sun, however, it did, blaze.

 Blazing in its powerful glow
 However, now sunlight flow
 Flowing down, giving light
 Casting shadows from, great height

 Flying towards solid ground
 Tiny atoms all, compound
 Within essences of bright blue
 Misty haze, how she grew

 Covering fields with dull mist
 Rain, however, it did persist.
 Pouring down gloomy day
 That sky now is dull, grey.

Misty Murky

On this misty, murky morn
Helmsmen pap's on his horn
In, that thick mist upon a cruise
A smokey trail he does, defuse.

Smoke comes out, boat flume
In that misty, murky gloom
Our captain, he does steer.
Rev up to another gear.

Down canal, it chugs away
Passing field of golden hay
Birds above are flying high
Within that murky, misty sky

Our helmsmen, cruises on
In that fog, he'll be, gone.
Chugging to another place
Down canal life's not a race.

Countryside Code

Always take your litter home
Deadly fields, bulls may roam
Careful of planted seeds
Please keep dogs on leads.

Always beware, risk! Of fire
Empty bottles do! Perspire
Farm machines leave alone.
Or your limbs are re-sewn.

Pothole lane, potholes found
So, beware of unsteady ground
Help streams keep them clean
Pickled cucumber stagnates green.

Please use all gates supplied
 Always follow countryside guide
 Be sure not to make much noise
 Self-reflections stop, then poise.

Enjoy our countryside to its full
 Whether it's sunny or worse, dull
 Use paths marked on your way
 See our wildlife all at play.

I hope this advice you follow
 See swallow, mind bunny hollow
 Another rhyme, one of Lee's
 Please beware of bees in trees.

Pothole Lane 1

Walking down Pothole lane
Stumble, pothole, I fall again,
Past field, a field of humps
My head now has two bumps.

No hay bails left to sit on
Cows ate them all gone
Empty pallets on straw, floor
Horse in field neighs for more.

No sugar lumps for that horse
Horse it shows no remorse
As it nipped me on my arm
This horse wears a tiny, charm,

Sitting in our countryside air
Field of green flows like hair
As I write this one last verse
On my toe tractor, reverse.

Pothole Lane 2

Walking down pothole lane
 Off to meet cows again
 With cows big long face
 Rambling to my secret place,

 Hearing sounds, countryside
 Birds flying off to hide
 Fluttering tiny black wings
 Buzzing bees, painful stings,

·In that barn I sit then, study
 Honestly its fairly muddy
 Friendly cows that I feed
 Constant munch, sheer greed

Within a misty sunny haze
 Sitting, writing how I gaze.
 Fluttering birds beautifully sing.
 Yes, for it is finally spring.

 Misty mist now descend
 Another day, finally end
 Walking back up pothole lane
 Tomorrow I'll be back again.

Noah's Ark

On canal boat Noah's Ark
Noah awoke like a lark
With larks, music sweet
Upon its two dainty feet

Noah listened to this sound
In those fields, all around
Was a grunt from Mr, Pig?
Lark fell off a narrow twig.

Noah then spotted a crow
As that crow flew solo
Noah's goat began to, but
Noah's boat, metal hut

Noah's boat still afloat
After butted by that goat
Then a sheep started, bleat
Bleat, bleat, continued sheep.

Now that peace has gone
Afternoon half-past one
Upon path close to Ark
Dog Chihuahua did a bark.

Noah, dog looked so rough
Shabby fur looked, a scruff,
Noah felt for that scruffy dog
Begging within boaters smog

Noah's smog drifting clear
Chihuahua he called it Deer
Deer now upon Noah's boat
Pig, dog, sheep plus goat

Canal Ramble

Down canal, I take a gamble
 In, my trainers start a ramble
Walking over fresh shale
Summer wind blows a gale.

Towards lock, I will stroll
As fish swim in a shoal
Heading up towards, lock
On our canal floats a sock

Weathers now changed to rain
Out, in open waters a pain
Wearing my puffy hood
Looking where heron stood

Herons thin, tall, long neck,
Continuing up on my trek
Doing up coat hood stud
Trainers splattered in mud.

Continuing in, my muddy trainers
Those ducks quacked, entertainers
It was all so very amusing
As boaters continued cruising

Over a bridge now on track
 On Monk's walk, I head back
Through trees so very green
 In our breezy summer sheen

Through a gate over, field
 Field though unconcealed
 Very open, gusty wind blows.
 Cold face, cheeks glows,

 Walking back up School Lane,
 It has been muddy yet again,
 Through that muddy sludge
 Has this mud got a grudge?

 Passing by a fishing gnome
 As I make my way home
 For now, I'm soaking wet
 Tomorrows same, you can bet

Navvy Men

Listening to chatty, cheap birds
Pen to paper wrote these, words
Thought about them, navvy men
Thinking back, way back then

How navvies dug canals so deep
Night times how they'd sleep
Out amongst bright stars
Plus, amazing red planet Mars

Bet navvies somewhat whacked
Those rocks they then all cracked
Another load of worthless rubble
Thrown upon farmers stubble

Taking many years to complete
Rubble now turned into peat
Water containment's, fishing lead
Plus, our unwanted bread.

Boaters Cruise

Down canal boaters cruise
Too much ale now they snooze
On that canal water, trickle
Sandwiches cheese with pickle,

Ladies with wine in hands,
Men drink from beer cans,
Down canal, that boat sways
All now, upon weeks, holidays,

From one side to another
Dad, son, or his brother!
Fairly, big, speaking Dutch.
Another beer far too much

Swerving upon their way
Enjoying a merry holiday
Another beer in their hands
Canal path lies, empty cans,

Paralytic upon boat sail
Cruise with too much ale
Local people all do frown,
On our canal, they cruise down.

Boaters' Smog

Down canal boaters slog
 Among thick horrid smog
 Churned up by boaters boat
 Keeping comfy in my coat

 That thick smog, how it rises
 Hired a boat from Enterprises
 Down canal its engine chug
 Those lovers both do hug.

 Wrapped up in a loving way
 Erratically narrow-boat sway
 Never mind great big lock,
 Into lock boat does knock

 Those two lovers overboard
 From that stern, both got floored
 Boat, however, sunken now
 My advice, check your bow.

Pleasant Pheasant

Pleasant pheasant peasant
In dark wood peasant, goes
It's not at all that pleasant
Unpleasant, peasant, shows

For he is mean, angry, unpleasant
Pheasant flutters lovely wings
Was that peasant after pheasant?
Unpleasant, peasant sings,

Peasant luring that pheasant in
That unpleasant peasant
Peasant drank a dram of gin
Wraps rest up for pheasants present.

Around a wood, peasant stagger
Shouting pleasant, pheasant present
Then a woodcock swagger
Watch out, pleasant pheasant,

Droppings dropped on that peasant
From pheasant not that pleasant
Then that pleasant pheasant
Sat on that unpleasant peasant present!

Green Meadow

Out across green meadow
 Early mist still lingers
 Over dandelions so yellow
 Grass points like fingers

 Upon smelling of dewy land
 Some say how very pleasant
 Like grains of tiny sand
 Owned by a local peasant

 A peasant with his shooter
 Scaring many local birds
 Upon his motor scooter
 Mist surrounds my words.

 Peasant now draws his gun.
 Again, mistiness does fall.
 Peasant, shooting, having fun.
 As within this mist, I crawl.

Misty Lee

Saw my friendly cow
 Called her Misty Lee
 Somewhat amazed how
 She remembered me

 Coming for a fuss
 Gave Misty Lee some hay
 Never does she cuss?
 Crossing farmyard way.

 A friendly cow Misty Lee
 Out of all those cows
 Always says moo to me
 Plus fussing she allows

 Tickling top of her head
 Also chin I gently pat
 Some cows moo with dread
 Misty Lee loves a chat.

 Misty Lee, friendly cow
 Friendliest I've ever met
 It truly is outstanding how
 Misty Lee does not forget.

Pothole Farm

Something was doing,
 Down at pothole farm
 Maybe trouble brewing
 Sounding like an alarm.

 Carrying on my walk
 Minding all those pots
 Blackbird gave a squawk
 Legs tied in tiny knots.

 Over, pothole, I carried on
 Fields now are very green.
 How summer's sun shone
 Blessed with a countryside scene

 Poly-tunnels that I pass
 Over hard ground, I tread
 Fields of meadow grass
 Watching out for electric thread

 Up towards new lake
 Water how it gently, flow
 Construction farmers make
 Irrigation seeds now all grow.

Meadows

Out across lovely meadows,
 Where tall, hay, grass grows
 Not a site for any bull-doze
 Where that green grass flows

 Flows about in a gentle breeze
 Pollinating for stripe bees
 Cows now graze, to please
 Pollen makes people sneeze.

Sneezing now is our local folk
 Most stood by fields, tall oak
 Some laugh or crack a joke,
 Now it rains, clothes all, soak

 A joke for, laugh it's not funny
 Rain now it was sticky sunny
 Bees buzzing searching honey
 Laughing aloud now Mr, Bunny

Bunny in our field does pout
 It was hot, so close to a drought
 Here he comes that lager lout
 Now in our meadow, time to get out.

Water Effect

On our canal pub reflects
  Bobbing about water effects
  Reflections of summer light
  As day turns into night,

  Eerie trees do, reflect
  Now bitten pesky insect
  Maybe horsefly in flight
  Now day turns tonight.

  That last light disappears
  Into local for some beers
  Upon water lovely, ripple
  Inside Inn, having a tipple

  Writing reflecting within
  Inside our busy pub, Inn.
  Now light gets ever dimmer.
  On our canal, lights last, shimmer.

Rainbow

Green, red, bright yellow
Underwater down below
Rainbow looks so mellow
Rising over farm meadow

Indigo, violet, lovely blue
Rainbows are for all to view
Over fields' cows, all moo
Orange, poetically, hard to do

A scene in which that rainbow glow
Shades green, red, bright yellow
Violet, blue, plus indigo
Orange I, am beat, lovely rainbow.

Sunny Nights

Sunny night, nearly at an end
Water, Sun, both do, blend,
That dog sits on boaters bow
From a bush cat, meow

Now, as that boat goes
Where it goes, nobody knows
Dog glares towards Sun
Knowing soon autumn no fun

Heading off on their way
In that last summer ray
On a towpath is a tiny bunny
Upon this day once so sunny.

Mirror Reflection

Reflection from cleaner mirror
 Looking at yourself much clearer
 Cleaner mirror once cobwebbed full
Finding out you are not so dull?

Cleaner mirror, now fresher life
 No more troubles, woes, or strife
 Now look in, inspect yourself
 Like, mirror fresh new health.

 Now clean around that dusty frame
 Ask mirror if it knows your name
 Although somewhat a bizarre situation
 Seeing into your mirror reflection.

Countryside Ode

Conversations bird's tweet
Sounds so, vocally sweet,
Occasional taps, woodpecker
Woodpecker is a noisy wrecker.

No doubt tapping using code
Tapping finding out its abode,
Chirping away now awaiting, reply
Maybe girl! Or maybe, a guy,

On enjoyable countryside walks
Spotting lots of sparrowhawks,
Chirping, tweeting, away
Like they do every day,

Plowed fields seeds, sown
Crow squawks with a groan,
Blackbird first flies into, bush
Second sparrow, then a Thrush,

Twittering, lovely sound
Hearing tweets all around,
Maybe it is our bird routine
Within fields freshly green.

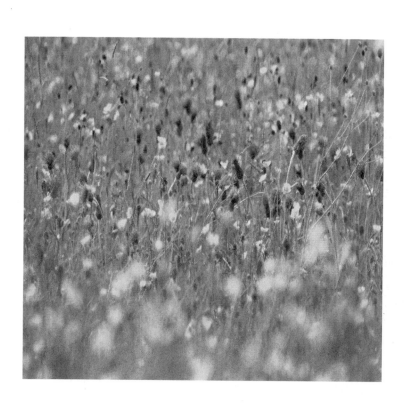

Massey Ferguson

Used to pull many a ton
Did old Massey Ferguson,
Roads now a pothole factor
Loved my Reddish tractor,

Its track-rod end, how it sways
Too many potholes nowadays,
Wobbly wheels got a SORN
Leather seating is very worn.

Reddish now extremely rusty
Tires also really crusty,
Flaking off here or there
One chunk landed in my hair.

I've scrapped, Reddish beast
Many mouths she has, feast,
Plowed, sewn plus shred
One last rev, Reddish dead,

I loved Reddish it, loved me
Around fields filled with glee,
Off to heaven or scrap yard
Reddish Ferguson worked hard.

Canal Moon

Over canal, moon it shone
Photos snapped five to one,
Underneaths water ripple
After indulging final tipple,

Underneaths waters deep
All fish now fast asleep,
Clouds drift across our moon
Wouldn't see this at noon,

Now that moon goes
Canal, ripples, water flows,
Rippling constantly on
Time is now, half-past one.

Rambling

Canal boats pulled, by a tug
Along, canal engine chug,
Down Canal now on its way
Too scrap yard, I must say.

Walking that old meadow path
Sheep all needing a bath,
With shabby coats of wool
Those sheep all look dull.

Carrying on my way
Infield, two horses neigh,
One's black, others white
Public footpath, bear right,

Autumn leaves fall too, ground
Swaying trees, lovely sound,
Field, however, grass infested
Cut it, farmer, I protested.

Another stile to contend
Will this walk ever end?
Graceful buzzard flying high
Within thermals of blue sky,

Another stile I will climb
I do hope you like this rhyme,
Crab apples lie on, muddy floor
Into darkness, you want more.

A mucky filthy pond lies near
Branches sharper than a spear,
Blood red leaves fall off trees
A rambling poem, one of Lee's,

Pleasant Pheasant flutters near
Wood pigeons I have a fear,
Around stile carry on walking
Hearing sound of birds squawking.

Tripping over a solid log
Imagine landing on a frog,
Through boggy marshland
This poem, gone underhand,

With each squelch I make
Marshland looks like a lake,
Another boat moves slowly
Now I'm praying very holy.

Small puddle it may seem
Under viaduct usually a stream,
To field where new seeds grow
Autumn day, north wind blow.

Autumn Breeze

Gusty trees, autumn breeze
No pollen to sneeze or wheeze,
Trees of leaves nearly bare
Squirrels scupper without care.

Looking out for winter wad
Through autumn leaves I plod,
Embracing this wildlife scene
Reminiscing, to trees, green.

Up tall tree squirrel climbs
Gathering nuts for winter times,
From giant oak grabbing nuts
Squirrels now gigantic, guts,

Another windy, gusty blow
Far up north, soon be snow,
Down trees squirrels descend
Another autumn close to its end

Night of Two Sunsets

As cows graze
Under, sunset sky,
Cloud's people gaze
Two sunsets apply.

Cows graze unaware
Of sunset scene,
Grazing without care
In pasture green,

Cows graze around
Sky like a choppy sea,
Not a single sound
Birds head off for tea,

Beautiful, quiet solitude
Time ticks slowly by,
Sunset so well-viewed
Poetically, I sigh.

Windmill

Windmill stood very still
Up on top of windmill hill,
Miller's name, simple Bill
Windmill blew, gave him a thrill.

Over days, even years
Windmill failed rusty, gears,
Windmill caused many fears
Bill stood alone, full of tears.

Out of windmill, not one grain
Causing Bill endless pain,
Even in damp pouring, rain
Rustic sound of a weather vane,

Suddenly lightning struck
Also striking passing duck,
People said, "Rotten luck."
Windmill fell on Bill's truck.

Bills windmill now has gone
No longer here to dwell on,
Carrying on, I scrambled on
As my friends have rambled on,

Ambling on down that lane
Overgrown like lions-mane,
Wonder if windmill built again
Think to myself, what a shame

Psycho Bee

Take a walk-up, psycho lane,
Telling you it is right again.
A very, meadow pleasant walk
Once heard a pheasant squawk.

Following signs showing, path
Watch out for that psychopath
Psycho killer loves fruits or nuts
Do watch out for his butts.

Keep walking! Do not stop
Watch out for, planted, crop.
Go as straight as can, be
But lookout, for, psycho bee.

Psycho! He once stood there.
It is dangerous, do take care.
Edge of field, bricks, are seen.
Psycho killer in, field green

In this meadow, I get lost
So bring a map at all cost
Such a mellow walk to do,
"Psycho bee, where are you?"

Autumn Haze

Birds chirp dirt, cheep
Bales of hay piled in, heap
Autumn, haze silly banter
In a paddock, she does canter.

Birds fly to different trees
Trees sway, gentle, breeze
Autumn tail swish, then sway
Flicking horrid flies away

Within fields, fields so green
Crows, crowing, so obscene
Cursing out plus much worse
Autumn neigh's final verse

Another field cows graze
A final kick off Autumn Haze
Clouds cover, setting, Sun
Autumn nights have begun.

Remembrance Poems
(Bonus Collection)

Remembrance Poem 1

In battle, those brave men fought
For our freedom, that was, brought
It cost their loved ones very dearly
That's why we have remembrance yearly
Remembering you in our thought

Remembrance Poem 2

As our heroes marched to Somme,
Those German Fokker s they did bomb
Falling bombs from bi-planes
As our heroes were making gains
350,000 heroic men killed
Trenches since have been filled.
Bloody battles, so much fighting
Must have been truly terrifying
Seeing friends or loved one die
Bombs dropped from, dark sky
During daytime or even night
Indeed this is a bloody insight.

Remembrance Poem 3

Those bloody cries of war
Shouting out once more
In those trenches, many men,
Men to whom we say amen

Bodies lay in those trenches.
For many days imagine stenches.
How those bloody ditches bled
Where hundreds of men lay dead

Move along gradually each day
With bibles at night, they'd pray
Hoping bloody war would go away
But those brave men had no say.

Carrying on, regardless of killing,
Army life so extremely chilling
No time to either sleep or eat
Up all day, up on their feet

Watching out for that enemy fire
As comrades burned up on, pyre,
With each shot comrade, downed
Another body, on pyre mound.

Can't imagine what it'd be like
Not knowing way enemy strike
Maybe by day or even by night
Or during shiny moonlight

That blood-red moon disappears
Looking back over many years
Remembering what granddad told
Thinking of brave young men so bold

Remembrance Poem 4

Caught within that enemy fire
Bodies lay strewn situation dire
Normandy beaches our heroic men
Never should war happen again

Bodies battered, bloody, bruised
Normandy beach, heroes, confused
Sandblasting in their eyes
No one heard our heroes' cries.

Barbed wire, fields' deadly mines
As they crossed those enemy lines
Bombed from above, shot from behind
If caught tortured, in camps confined

Non-stop, bloody confrontation
Loved ones waited at a London station
Many heroes sadly did not survive
Wear a poppy keep remembrance alive

Remembrance Poem 5

To battlefields, brave men went far away
Not knowing what price they would pay
Into deep trenches brave, soldiers dug
With them, no loved ones to now hug.

Fighting for freedom, fighting for a friend
Praying this bloody war was at an end
Within trenches bloodshed brave tears
No time to show their feelings or fears

It was their lives they were fighting for
During our first also second world war
So wear a poppy with utmost pride,
Praying, a third war, we will never slide.

Twenty two, Nine Lady

Twenty-two nine, lovely lady arrive,
 In a mini car that she does drive
 Smile every morning felt very warm
 Without her around doesn't feel norm
 Walking together, we'd both chat
 Chat about this, then talk about that
 Lady is a friend always on my mind
 Twenty-two nine, lady best you can find

Train Journey

On rails train, does trundle
Ticket prices cost a bundle
Upon train, I grabbed a seat
Man opposite sips whiskey neat
He's crumpling up his paper
Reading aloud political caper
Or indeed celebrity deceased
Tell you what papers creased
Next stop that chaps off
Fowl chap made me cough.

Now a wailing baby cries,
Trains now have few flies,
Seating though fairly plush
Trouble is people crush,
I'm all right sitting at a table,
Whizzing under, electric cable
Baby wails! Flies flying
Wish that baby stops crying,
Two more stops left to do
Before my destination Crewe

Now though, I'll take a nap
Upon my head fly, I zap
No rest for wicked, me,
Porter delivers a cup of tea
Tea's on trains very weak
Also had to take a leak
It's small, claustrophobic
Toilet stench is anaerobic
Urine drips everywhere
Over here, over there,

Thank goodness baby's gone
Scientific geek, always one,
Notes on mutilated body parts
Wish he'd gone to other carts?
Depressing me, getting on my wick
Pictures in papers so, very sick
One of those big-headed chaps
Teas tipped over hate mishaps
Gone over his exam paper
Nearly end of this rail caper

Now, free of scientific boffin
Table opposite lies wicker coffin
Surely things can't get any worse
A voice from, coffin starts to curse
Another train, a different week
Outside weathers turned bleak
Don't know what else to do
Relived to get off at Crewe
Now alas trains broke down
Our train driver dressed as a clown!

Lapley Church

Hearing church bells chime
Ending of our summer, time
Autumn trees in surround
Mellow grass in church ground

Covering people passed before us
No longer here to curse or cuss
Loved ones never forgot,
With gravestones on each plot

Memories last forever, more
Memories of loved ones you adore
It's a church where I was, christened,
To our vicar, people listened

A final chime of summer strike
Home I'll cycle on my bike
This church I'll never forget
Choir within sings a final duet.

Climate Change

What is occurring within ice caps?
Once full of ice, now full of gaps
Global warming, climate change
Temperature, soaring out of range!
Northern, southern regions, cold
In too many countries, this land sold
Sold for oil with economics deep
As those icebergs silently weep
Seas build up more land gone
Icebergs melted as our sun shone
Those icebergs will be no more
Continents vanished to our seafloor,
All of our planets living in rack and ruin
Trouble is though its all our do-in

Water

Water's something that we drink
We get this from our sink
Turn that tap watch it go
Into a glass or cup does flow

H20 is its proper name
Call it water albeit, same
In this water bath or shower
Sometime in there for an hour

Water, we do take for granted
Like on flowers, all well-planted
Water's something we abuse
Water's something that we use.

Without water would not survive
We need water to keep alive
Water is all around us
Helps us clean car or bus

Water is vital not to waste
With chlorine in, a weird taste
So friendly water we say thanks
Thank you water, in water tanks

IT/Space

From outer space, It came,
No integrity to Its name.
It has no religion or race
That, It without a face

No one knew much about
Only that It did shout
Annoyance to worldly things
Plus destruction, human beings

Seeing Earth close to disaster
Losing control much faster
Humans should work together
No matter what our weather?

It went back into its spaceship
It shouted out one last tip
Stop your destructive ways
Then you'll live infinite days.

Virus

"Achoo" oh God bless you
Now I'm on my way
Upon this Earthly zoo
On someone else you spray
Oh god bless you, sir
Into your eyes, I'm in
For a second eye may blur
At least I didn't go in a bin
Oh God bless you
I'm multiplying yes
Now you're in a queue
Rest in peace, God bless!"

Coronavirus

Smaller than a millipede
Clinging onto surfaces
Causing so much villainy
Touching skin on your faces
Can't spot me, but I see you
Go around spreading germs
Honestly, you have no clue
Smaller than earthworms
I can fly around, your air
Spreading me all around
Some humans do not care
I am mute so have no sound
Coronavirus, so deadly
You will never see me
This my deadly medley
Coronavirus, I will not flee.

Lockdown

Why don't people understand?
A lockdown means lockdown
Theirs no heading off to sand
Nor loitering around town

Why don't people bother?
A lockdown means lockdown,
Don't they care about another?
Or are they fooling, like a clown

Why don't people listen?
A lockdown means lockdown
Our night sky, stars glisten
Like Corona Borealis, crown

Why don't people care?
A lockdown means lockdown
They give an alien glare
See loads of them around.

Why are people aggressive?
A lockdown means lockdown
It is not at all impressive
Lockdown, not a showdown

Why are people selfish?
A lockdown means lockdown
Eating loads of shellfish
Pulled up before they drown

Why can't people be nice
A lockdown means lockdown
We only have one roll of dice
Before reaper comes around

Viral virus

Are we free from this viral virus?
That's a question we must ask us?
Are we still spreading that disease?
I suppose to virus its just cheese
No matter what you do it is there
It could be lurking, anywhere
Touching your computer keys
How it spreads corona disease
You think it's gone disappeared
Now that R might have cleared
Going down ever so slow
R uptake, graphs, do flow
That virus has no boundaries
Office worker or in foundries
Was so pleasant, living in, past
This virus spreads so very fast.

Poems by

Lee Fones

All poetry © Copyrighted poet Fones 2020

Many thanks to all the wonderful
photographers and artist.

Photos by
Bexter Robb
Gaz Williams
Dave Heyhoe
Ray Cowley
Alan Poulson
Lorrette Fletcher
Alexandra Nixon
Alex Smart (RIP)
KL Lowde
Julie France
Ade Preece
Russ Whitingham
Clara Jacubs
Emma Shepherd
Carol Ann Langford

Drawings by
Emma Shepherd

Printed in Poland
by Amazon Fulfillment
Poland Sp. z o.o., Wrocław